WHO WAS CONFUCIUS?

Ancient China Book for Kids
Children's Ancient History

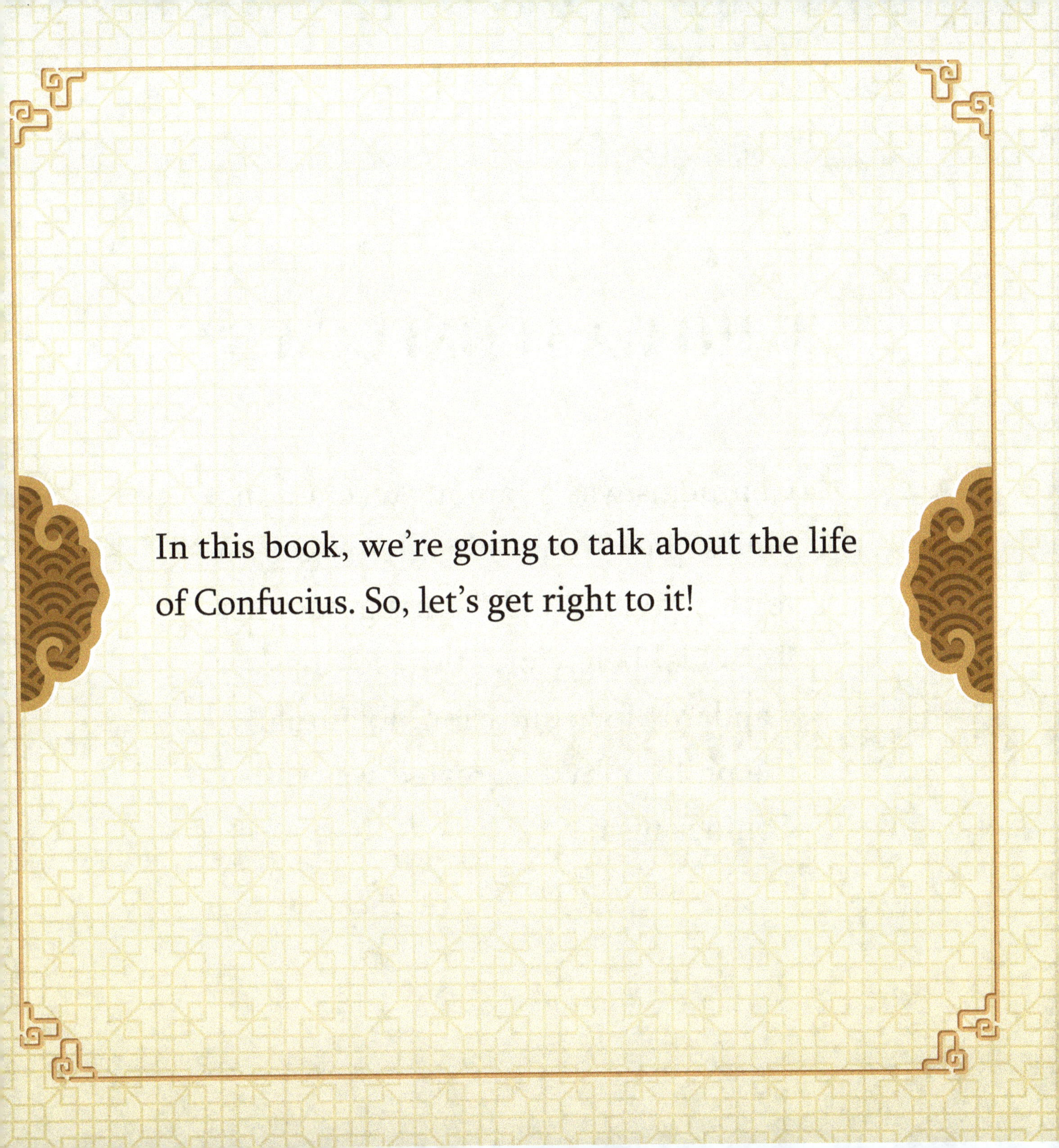

In this book, we're going to talk about the life of Confucius. So, let's get right to it!

WHO WAS CONFUCIUS?

Confucius was a famous teacher and philosopher from China. He is known for his sayings and for his guidelines for social behavior. His teachings set standards for education. Eventually, the philosophy he created was called Confucianism.

Confucius Sculpture

Confucius Temple

It became the official philosophy of the leaders of China and influenced their policies during three dynasties—the Han Dynasty, the Tang Dynasty, and the Song Dynasty.

HIS EARLY LIFE

It's believed that Confucius was born around 551 BC in the former state of Lu in China, which is now the province of Shandong, also called Shantung. However, there are no historical records of him until about four centuries after he died.

Confucius Statue
先師孔子行教像

Because he became a famous, "larger than life" figure, some details about his life may have become blended with fictional stories that tell of his legend. Confucius is mentioned in the Historical Records written by Sima Qian so some details about his life are noted.

However, some historians distrust the accuracy of this book, and have debated the details of the story of his life, since it was written so many years after his death.

Temple of Confucius

Qufu

It's thought that he grew up in the town of Qufu. Some documents claim that he was born into a royal family that was part of the Chou Dynasty, but more than likely this isn't true. His father was a soldier by the name of Kong He. He died when Confucius was only three years of age.

After his father's death, Confucius and his mother lived on the edge of poverty at times. Despite this, Confucius, also known as Kong Qui, became part of the middle class in China.

萬世師表

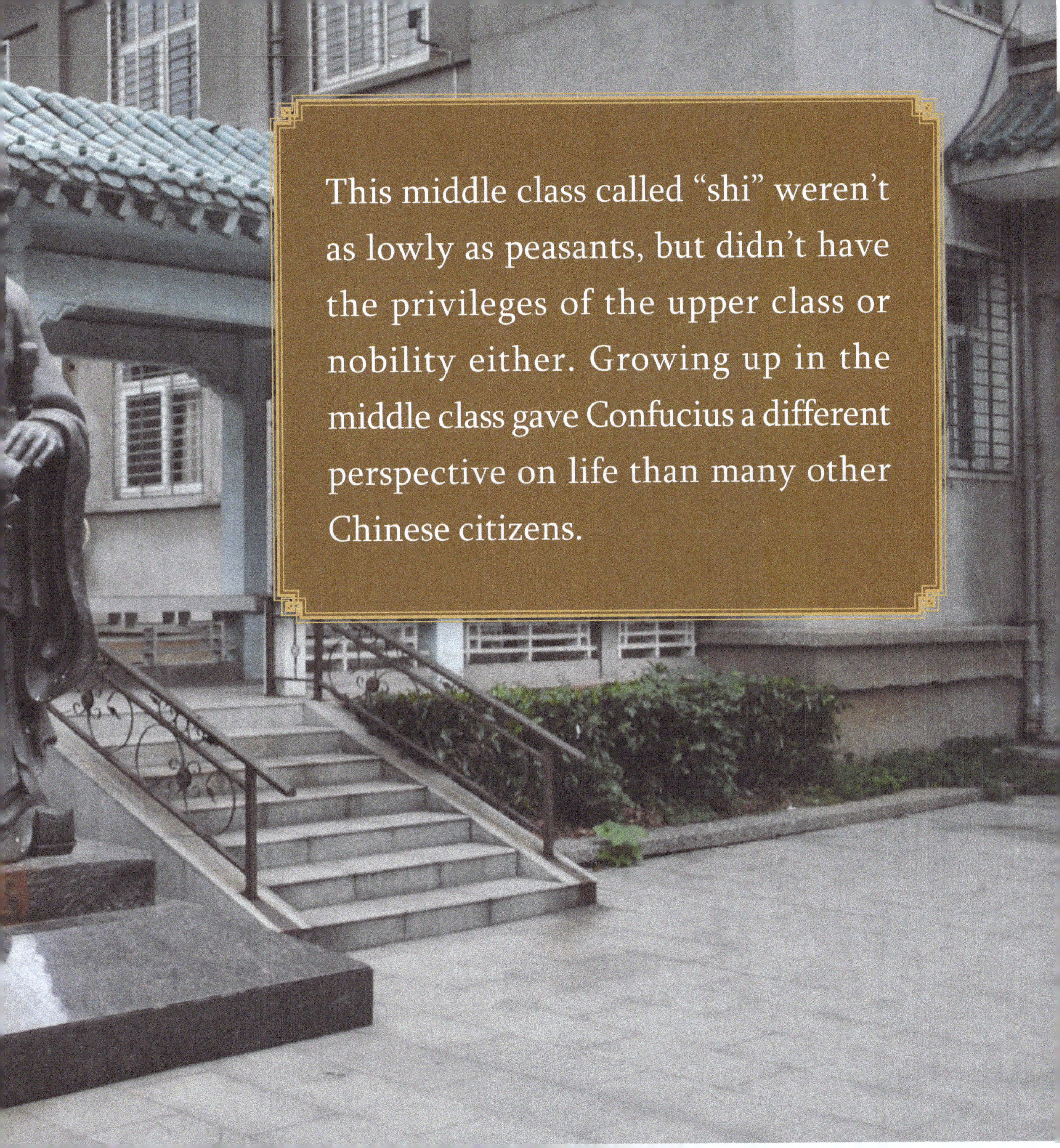

This middle class called "shi" weren't as lowly as peasants, but didn't have the privileges of the upper class or nobility either. Growing up in the middle class gave Confucius a different perspective on life than many other Chinese citizens.

He felt that people should be able to improve their social status based upon their hard work and their talents. Because of these changes in society and the political climate, China was in a state of crisis during his life. His destiny as a teacher and philosophical leader was perfect for when he came of age.

萬
孔聖降生二千五百□
公曆一千九百□
香港孔教學院院　主
副

However, he didn't begin his career as a wise teacher. For a while, he worked as a shepherd and then became a clerk. Little by little he got into the Chinese government. He governed a small town and then became a chief advisor to the top leaders.

He was promoted to a position as the Public Works Director for the Prince of the state of Lu in 503 BC. By 501 BC, he was the Justice Department Director.

全国重点文物保护单位
曲阜鲁国故城
中华人民共和国国务院
一九六一年三月四日公布
山东省人民委员会立
State of Lu

He traveled all over China for his positions and he was once thrown in prison because he was mistaken for someone else. Legend says that he calmly played music on his lute until the authorities realized they had made a horrible mistake and released him. After his many travels, he settled down in his home city and founded a school.

His mission at the school was to teach his students the wisdom of their ancient ancestors. Rich and poor students were both welcome to attend his school. Confucius didn't consider himself to be a creator of this wisdom. Instead, he considered himself to be a communicator of the moral principles of the ancients.

Remains of carriages and horses

A TIME OF CHANGE

During this time in Chinese history, the Chou Empire had maintained a supreme level of rule over the provinces for five centuries. Different Chinese states were beginning to question this authority. The principles that had been held true by the ancient Chinese ways were starting to decline, which means that people weren't paying attention to them anymore.

Confucius was concerned about these changes. He believed in the traditions of the ancients as well as compassion toward his fellow man. "Loving others" was a core principle within his teachings. This principle was called "ren." He believed in what we know of as "The Golden Rule," which essentially says to treat others in the way that you would want to be treated by them.

Altar of Confucius

As far as his political beliefs, Confucius felt that leaders should lead by example. He believed that those in power should practice self-discipline as well as humility. He felt strongly that true leaders "practice what they preach" and set an example for their followers.

He taught his students to live a life of virtue and good will toward others. Confucius felt that the best way to get the population to follow laws was for their leaders to obey the law and set a positive example for the citizens to observe and be inspired by.

明倫堂

大學之道在明明德在新民在
止於至善知止而后有定定
后能靜靜而后能安安而
慮慮而后能得物有本末
終始知所先後則近道矣古之
欲明明德於天下者先治其國
欲治其國者先齊其家欲
家者先脩其身欲脩其身
正其心欲正其心者先誠其
欲誠其意者先致其知致
格物物格而后知至知至
意誠意誠而后心正心正而后
身脩身脩而后家齊家齊而后
國治國治而后天下平自
以至於庶人壹是皆以脩
本其本亂而末治者否矣
厚者薄而其所薄者厚末
也　後學趙孟頫書

Tainan Confucian Temple

In addition to the principles of Confucianism, the students in his classes were taught how to write calligraphy and how to shoot arrows in archery class. They were also taught music and mathematics. How to drive a chariot and how to participate in ancient rituals were also part of the curriculum.

Confucius expected his students to understand how to conduct their lives with honesty. The values of generosity toward others and the appropriate conduct, rituals, and manners were also emphasized as core principles. He felt that these traditional values, taught by the ancients many centuries before, should be part of the fabric of society.

Tablet of Confucius

Confucius

In addition to modeling these virtues himself, Confucius taught his principles with short, simple phrases that could be interpreted in many ways. His sayings were very memorable so his students were able to keep them in mind and pass them along to their children and grandchildren. If you've ever heard the term "Confucius say" and then a quote after it, you'll realize that many of his sayings and stories have lasted until modern times since he taught them over 2,000 years ago.

HIS WRITINGS

In addition to being an advisor to leaders in the government and a wise and respected teacher, Confucius was also a writer. During his time as a teacher, he began to write many different books.

Confucius

He wrote:

- The Book of Odes, which was a collection of poetry
- The Book of Documents, which was a history of China
- The Spring and Autumn Annals, which was a history of the state of Lu
- The Book of Changes, which was a collection of essays on how to find hidden knowledge using rituals and foretelling the future

Unfortunately, none of his books set down his philosophy. During his life his philosophy was not widely accepted. About 30 years after his death, his students began to compile his sayings and stories into a book called the Analects. Later, three other books were written about his teachings. The first book was called the Mencius, the second was called the Great Learning, and the third was called the Doctrine of the Mean.

Temple of Confucius

Confucian Temple

These four books together are thought of as the classics of Confucianism. It was through his students' work that his principles became well known and became the official philosophy and religion of China from the beginning of the Han Dynasty in 206 BC forward and still have an influence today.

In order to become a civil servant in China, a citizen had to pass an examination that was based on his principles. The leaders of China strongly supported his philosophy because it was centered around a strong government and respect for authority.

校訓
誠正勤樸
劉真

A SIMPLE PHILOSOPHY

The basic tenets of Confucianism may seem simple,
but they aren't easy to practice in daily life.

Confucius believed that:

- People should treat each other with respect and kindness
- Each person should practice good manners, be polite, and maintain daily rituals
- Fathers and mothers should have strong morals and practice ethical behavior
- A man would only be at his best if he had the qualities of honesty, goodness, and loyalty
- People should practice moderation in everything they do
- The central government should be strong and organized

LATER LIFE

When he was 51 years old, Confucius left his government position. He was saddened that the leaders in the government had not accepted and followed his teachings. He traveled and taught his philosophy as he went from city to city. He continued to teach his devoted students in his final years and he passed away in 479 BC.

坊磨家展
孔家故井
Confucius Hometown Park

SOME FAMOUS SAYINGS

Confucius had many famous sayings and he became so influential over time, that there are probably many sayings and stories that are attributed to him that were never said by him. Here are some of the ideas he taught his students.

Our greatest virtue is not in never stumbling, but in rising again every time we fall.

↳ Everything around us has beauty, but not everyone can see it.

↳ When anger overtakes you, think of the consequences of your actions.

↳ A person who has made a mistake and doesn't correct it, is making another mistake.

↳ Choose a job you're passionate about, and you will live a life you love.

Awesome! Now you know more about the life of Confucius. You can find more Ancient History books from Baby Professor by searching the website of your favorite book retailer.

周 敦 颐 铜 像
（1017—1073）

Visit
BABY PROFESSOR
EDUCATION KIDS
www.BabyProfessorBooks.com
to download Free Baby Professor eBooks
and view our catalog of new and exciting
Children's Books